Light in Dark Spaces

poems by

Margery Hutter Silver

Finishing Line Press
Georgetown, Kentucky

Light in Dark Spaces

Copyright © 2024 by Margery Hutter Silver
ISBN 979-8-88838-814-3 First Edition
All rights reserved under International and Pan-American Copyright Conventions. No part of this book may be reproduced in any manner whatsoever without written permission from the publisher, except in the case of brief quotations embodied in critical articles and reviews.

ACKNOWLEDGMENTS

My thanks to the publications in which these poems originally appeared.

Paper Nautilus: 'Word Game"
Third Wednesday: "Lapis," "Free to Overlook," "Restoration"
Muddy River Poetry Review: "Sleight of Mind," "Morning Call"
Journal of Undiscovered Poets: "It's Not the End," "Drawing Birds at Twilight"
Ibbetson Street Press: "Collision"
The Somerville Times: "Along the River"
Invisible Sidewalk Poetry: "Small Outcry"

I want to express my appreciation to Barbara (bg) Thurston, whose patient guidance and suggestions made this book possible. Barbara Helfgott Hyett has my deepest gratitude for inspiring me, challenging me, and making me into a poet. Special thanks to Becky Kennedy, whose insightful critiques have enriched my writing.

Publisher: Leah Huete de Maines
Editor: Christen Kincaid
Cover Art: c1985 Natalie Alper. All rights reserved.
Author Photo: Linda Taylor Davis
Cover Design: Elizabeth Maines McCleavy

Order online: www.finishinglinepress.com
also available on amazon.com

Author inquiries and mail orders:
Finishing Line Press
PO Box 1626
Georgetown, Kentucky 40324
USA

Contents

Our Words 1
Sleight of Mind 2
Drawing Birds at Twilight 3
Autumn Blaze 4
Sunday Morning 5
Snow Scene at Night 6
Soaking in Moonlight 7
Light in Dark Spaces 8
Along the River 9
Oak Leaf 10
Scent of a Rowboat 11
I Have Known These Stairs 12
The Pretzel Factory 13
Waste Not, Want Not 14
Mining Hurt 15
Great-Grandma's Kitchen 16
Boy at 14 17
Tapestry 18
Sip of Life 19
Time and Travel 20
Love Villanelle 23
Seasons of Sin 24
Lapis 25
Blue-Footed Boobies 26
Collision 27
Running 28
Tyler's Mind 29
It's Not the End 30

Christ in Cyberspace	31
Free to Overlook	32
Image of Your Departure	33
Aquifer	34
Cremains	35
Touch of Love	36
Sometimes	37
Word Game	38
Morning Call	39
Shorty's Ears	40
Snow Scene at Dawn	41
The Rodent	42
Small Outcry	44
Renegade Hand	45
Poet's Block	46
Sweet Birch	47
Pine	49
For the Bathroom Ant	50
The Quilter	51
Restoration	52

This book is dedicated to my fellow poet, the late Ruth Margolin Silin, mentor, muse, and cherished friend, and to my daughters, Althea and Julie, and my grandsons, Casey, Tyler, Riley, and Azar, for always believing in me, no matter how many birthdays I have.

Our Words

Our words are sand,
gritting tears.
Our words are honey,
sweetening our tongues.
Our words are water,
melting winter,
soothing rough rocks
in the early river.
Our words carom heart to heart,
the distance from lip to ear,
as far as old age and beyond.

Sleight of Mind

My memory of why
I walked to the kitchen
stays behind
in the dark bedroom.
Yet my hand opens
the refrigerator
as if it recalls
that much, but should
I reach for eggs,
English muffins?
If I go back
to bed, can I
find the missing
memory? And will
I then remember
just where I put
the thread I need
to mend my life?

Drawing Birds at Twilight

Drawing birds with charcoal pencil,
light strokes for clouded sky at dusk.
Rub with index finger to flatten gray
as far as the horizon.
Press hard for thin twisted lines,
trees that silhouette black against the sky.

Next the chickadee. Erase gray,
show the breast's white plumpness.
Press hard for black cap and throat, then
add the feeder's peg, targeted for a downward
dive to dine.

The titmouse, not so bold,
skirrs in and out the top branches.
Shade him grayer than the sky.
Sketch proud crest tufts and
bear down for round black eyes,
scouting for sunflower seeds below.

When the downy woodpecker swoops
in, take care to capture the symmetry
of two white-dotted black lines
that follow the sides of his wide
white center strip. He taps
a thick branch as he prepares
to snatch his share.

Please, do not darken twilight
to opaque night that hides
the birds till dawn.

Autumn Blaze

Flash of cardinal
among dusty sparrows
foraging in brittled oak leaves.
Above, crimson radiates
three matching maples
at the garden's edge.
Six dark-red mums
disrupt the regiments of yellow,
electrify my senses.
I will remember these red blazes
in gray February.
They heat my blood.

Sunday Morning
after Roethke

Slanted sun dries the egg yolk
on our plates, rewarms our coffee,
seeps through the newspapers
screening our bed-raggled faces.

Beneath the table, my toe touches
your shin, the hairs that travel higher.
The sun deserts the cluttered table.
Your sports page rustles to the floor.

We tunnel into our rumpled sheets,
jumble lips and fingers. *The mouth
asks. The hand takes.* Our breath
quickens, in the high noon of sighs.

Snow Scene at Night

The streetlamps throw diamonds
on the nighttime snow.
Yesterday's puddle
gleams, slick with ice.
I take in the biting air
as greedily as I lap
cold water from a mountain spring in May.

Soaking in Moonlight

Two alone, shirts and shorts shed,
we soak in moonlight
on the rough wood of a hot tub's edge,
on a deck above a silent meadow.
In daylight our ears
welcome bird song,
the rustle of grass
as a snake passes.
At night we hear only
the swoop of a bat,
an owl's distant hoot.
You take my hand. We slide
into the moon-dyed water,
warm-blooded fish, no scales
to armor us against the slippery
invitation of each other's skin.

Light in Dark Spaces
after Yehuda Amichai

The power was out. Wind shook
tree limbs like a terrier worrying
a bone. My husband laid out
his flashlights. Three
Maglites made moons
on a mirror. An emergency
lantern flashed orange.
His favorite, the Squid, pointed
tentacles upward so its tiny bulbs
sequined the ceiling.
Hip to hip on the couch,
we toasted our festival of lights.
Mirrors, wine glasses glimmered.
Reflections filled dark spaces.

Along the River

The full moon
silvers the winding Charles on our
left. We round a curve; its brightness
mocks Boston's somber brownstones.
Back and forth it seems to fly, too
huge, too heavy with light
to be so nimble.

Oak Leaf

One leaf, autumn brown, finely veined,
clings to a rough oak branch,
stem taut with determination.
As the oak bends, tosses,
the leaf hangs tight,
through icy gusts, pelting rain,
and the weighted snow of winter.

So why now, in May,
does the leaf loose its hold?
Perhaps a rustle of feathered wings
whispers the hope of spring?

Scent of a Rowboat

Warmed wood, soft lapping,
my face drinking sun,
I watch my father's back.
His sweat-cured bucket hat,
banded with fishhooks,
slouches on his blond hair.
He pulls a red bandanna
from the wicker fishing creel
at his feet, daubs his forehead,
cheeks, mouth; his crisp
mustache never moves.
He lifts his pole, an arc of line,
earthy worm strikes water.

On nights I wait for sleep,
I fish behind my eyes,
boat soaked in lake water,
my measured breaths,
sun-touched sheets, whiff of
my father's shirt—sweat,
cigarette smoke, Old Spice.
I rock into sleep.

I Have Known These Stairs

The bounce on my mother's shoulder
as she carried me up to my crib.
The splinters in my knees
when I first crawled to the top,
and screamed for Mommy.
The bump of my knapsack,
in the rush to shed my school dress,
grab my roller skates, speed
away, around the block.
I never dreamed I would have a dream,
in the deep sleep of puberty,
throw off my comforter,
spread my arm-wings to the air,
fly free—on my own—fall,
strike every one of those weary stairs.

The Pretzel Factory
> *Pretzels were created around 610 BC in Italy*
> *by a monk who folded strips of dough*
> *to look like arms crossed in prayer.*

Every weekday,
after her father enlisted in the Army,
she crossed the street to the pretzel factory.
She fled her mother's tears and scolding,
her little brother's stormy tantrums
her own fears for her father.
In the long shed behind the Krugers' house,
six women wearing white aprons
and red hair scarves stood behind
a belt that moved ropes of dough,
like clay snakes from kindergarten.
When she walked in the door,
they looked up and smiled,
but the only sound was the click, click
of the dough machine. It repeated, like the
sound of worry beads, or rosaries.
With two quick movements each woman
folded a dough-snake into a pretzel,
into a prayer.

Waste Not, Want Not

Unwrapped bars of Ivory soap
lined her linen closet shelves.
They dried hard, lasted longer,
and stretched her budget.
She dissolved scraps of soap
in water, rainbowed the
mixture with food coloring,
so we could finger-paint
on rainy days with wild smears
of cerulean, vermilion, sunshine.
Today I pressed a scrap of Dove
tight against a new bar, until
I held a mother and daughter
spoon-sleeping in my palm.

Mining Hurt

Your hurt vein is buried deep
like the black mines under
our company-owned house
in a decaying anthracite town.

Sooty men dynamited black nuggets,
filled carts headed to the dusky coal breakers
silhouetted against the stark mountains,
barely visible in the grayed sunshine.

Your words explode like dynamite,
hurl angry blame from buried depths.
Jagged shards travel to my heart,
hot shrapnel that brings no warmth.

Great-Grandma's Kitchen

I hurried down the long front stairs, then passed
the silent parlor where Great-Grandma lay
in a dark pine box and the heavy sweet smell
of lilies drifted through the hall. In the dining
room, where the long table was set with the best
dishes, I smelled ham baking in the kitchen and heard
the clink of pans and the chop-chop of the big
knife against the cutting board.

It was very warm in the kitchen. Great-Grandma's
old scarred rocker was still in the corner
where she sat when we visited.
She always asked how old I was.
You'd think she could remember that I was eight.
I didn't like to hug her; she had no teeth
and smelled funny—like her ugly old cat.
Now I smelled only ham and
chopped onion.

I climbed into the rocker, glad she wasn't here.
I watched Grandma twirl a pie plate on her fingertips
as she trimmed the crust. Soon the scent
of apples drifted out of the old coal oven.

Grandpa George came into the kitchen
blowing his nose into his big white handkerchief;
his eyes were rimmed with red.
"Reverend Ulrich is here," he announced. "It's time."
While the women took off their aprons
and wiped their hands and faces,
I rubbed my eyes hard. I could not make tears,
but my eyes became red and wet.
I took Grandpa's hand and walked to the parlor.

Boy at 14

And the words stick in his throat like
the heavy phlegm of a winter cold.
It had been easy to spit out the anger.
"I hate you."
"You don't love me."

Now he struggles to push the bolus
of truth past his strong young teeth.
"I am ashamed."
"I am embarrassed."
"I am afraid."

Tapestry

Beauty woven in the front.
The back side, an understory
of the family's gnarled intentions,
tangled lies, knots and secrets.

Perfect, the tapestry we show on the wall.
Hidden, the flaws, the mistakes that save
us from God's wrath.

Sip of Life

Skirts way up, laugh in the grass, *let it all go, life!*
Blondie, I was, just one wanton lowlife.
Although sins pricked my spine, I said, *Never*
mind, did you expect a whiter-than-snow life?
But wine and song grew stale and emptiness grew
like weeds in my meaningless faux life.
Her voice in my head, my grandmother said,
Look inside for the true path to know life.
Thus, Blondie was shed and Margie came through
to plant a hoe-your-own-row life.

Time and Travel

> *And love is but an inn upon life's way.*
> Jose Santos Chocano

I.
Seventy years ago
our friendship began.
We were very different.
You were petite.
I was tall for thirteen.
You loved field hockey and basketball,
hated chemistry and math.
I was an A student,
except for gym and field hockey.
You went to Temple Israel.
I went to St. John's.
My home was busy and raucous,
with two younger siblings
and two black Labs.
Your home on Miner Street
was a calm, quiet haven.
Somehow we became
what you called, "bestest friends."

II.
The blue '46 Studebaker
was your sixteenth birthday gift,
a hand-me-down from your dad.
And we began to travel.
We cruised to Harveys Lake,
to show off
our new two-piece bathing suits,
which only got wet when we swam
to the warm, scratchy raft,
where our boyfriends waited.
Turning the Studebaker's sassy
headlights toward Scranton,
we sampled our first jazz
with Cab Calloway
at the Starlight Ballroom.

And in our pursuit of sophistication,
we secretly drove to hear Gussie sing
dirty songs at her eponymous roadhouse.
The highlight of our senior year was
a pilgrimage to Bethlehem—PA—
for dates with real college men
at Lehigh. So grown up,
such freedom (although
my mother insisted we stay
with her cousin—*absolutely no hotel!*).

III.
In our non-traveling years,
miles away from each other,
we held together by phone—through our marriages,
our children's foibles and triumphs,
your divorce, my husband's death.

IV.
Then we began to travel again.
We learned tango in Argentina.
At least you did.
My partner had to *drag* me across
the dance floor.
We fished for piranha in the Amazon,
where Woolly Monkeys invaded
our boat and stole our bait
while a sloth watched from a tree limb.
In Antarctica we smelled the penguin colonies
from our boat miles away.
Once on land, we stood in silence,
letting the curious tuxedoed birds
inspect us strange animals.
Even now I see
the view through our porthole
as our small ship sailed between
two shimmering glaciers,

silvered by the light of the full moon
that guided us through the passage.

V.
Now I sometimes travel
to your retirement community
hundreds of miles from my home.
More often we talk on the phone.
Your conversation travels back
to Miner Street and dinners
at your family's table,
where we stifled our giggles
at your father's jokes,
lest your mother give us "the look."
You talk about cruising
in the Studebaker to Harveys Lake,
about your boyfriend, who had
a fistfight one night with a rival
on your front lawn,
and about my boyfriend,
who has had three wives and ten children.
"I guess you dodged that bullet," you say.
We don't giggle any longer.
Our laughter is more resonant.
It sometimes catches in our throats.
I try to bring up our adventures
in Antarctica or the Amazon.
You tell me you remember,
but I'm not sure. You always
go back to Miner Street
and cruising in the Blue Studebaker
seventy years ago.

If this is the only direction
you can travel now,
of course, I will go with you.

Love Villanelle

I once believed in gentle love romantic
unfolding sweetly in its own time.
I cannot stay the course when things turn frantic.

Perhaps the difference is semantic.
For some a love is drama, chaos, heat.
I once believed in gentle love romantic.

Sometimes my emotions grow gigantic.
My breaths come rapid; heartbeats happen fast.
I cannot stay the course when things turn frantic.

My love is sometimes steady, sometimes antic.
I run from love that hits me like a storm.
I once believed in gentle love romantic.

It's like a winter-sailing transatlantic.
The waves grow high; then I am up and down.
I cannot stay the course when things turn frantic

I wake in horror from a dream bacchantic.
I panic when my passion burgeons strong.
I once believed in gentle love romantic.
I cannot stay the course when things turn frantic.

Seasons of Sin
> *Sins that were green last spring*
> *dried out over the summer*
> —Yehuda Amichai

Young sins, unripe horse chestnuts,
pricked my spine; grass stains
labeled the back of my blouse:
Forever damned.

My autumn sins, dried chrysanthemums,
weightless as milkweed puffs,
float through my mind,
like blessings.

Lapis

My lapis earring,
unfathomable
blue-lit lake,
alone in your box.
Your mate was lost
in cynical sheets
in an airport Marriot
with my high school friend.
His flight delayed,
an invitation to lunch,
our long-lurking lust.

Lapis lazuli,
Minerva's stone.
But I am not wise.

Blue-Footed Boobies

On a Galapagos lava ledge,
A pair of boobies dance
a mating minuet.
Long pointed beak toward
the sky, the male spreads
his wide white wings,
slowly raises a bright
blue foot, lowers it
to the earth, lifts the
other. The female responds,
mirroring every move.
They rub necks, nibble
each other's beaks.
He whistles, she moans.

A booby parent takes its turn,
warming a large chalk-blue
egg with its feet. Waiting for food
its mate will bring back,
it sits in the middle of a rock-strewn
path while tourists file past.
The booby watches with dark-ringed
eyes, but does not move.
The Portuguese named the bird Bobo,
Stupid, because it does not fear humans.

On a black volcanic bank,
hundreds of boobies gather.
Suddenly, as one, they rise,
flatten their feathers to sleek
body missiles, and dive, raising
a fountain of crystal drops
and silver fish—dive again,
and again, then, catapulting
from the water,
trailing a curtain
of liquid ribbons, they fly
home to their mates.

Collision

Iron hard and hot, the universe ends.
Slippery asphalt highway, unforgiving oak.
Stars strike my forehead, crack bone,
rip through dura mater, gray matter.
flashing orbs, medieval maces, spin,
spark thalamic; random axons pulse.
Fingers grab—haphazard.
My eyes dance, yet cannot see.

Running
after Mary Oliver

The knobs and points of all she owned
shaped the deep green garbage bag
she dragged behind her as she ran.
The bag bumped through a pool
of rainwater and one black shoe
slid unnoticed through its plastic skin
into the dark wetness. No one
rescued the sodden shoe
and set out to find its high-heeled mate.
And she kept on running, pulling
her life behind her into the night,
where time lies shattered.

Tyler's Mind

My grandson cannot speak or eat.
He's twenty-one, cheeks
rough with black whiskers.
On his back, a child's pack
hides the pump that snakes
liquid life through a tube,
a new umbilical cord
that enters near his navel.
But he runs, he smiles, he weeps
and sometimes fetches
The Little Engine That Could,
pulls me to the couch
to read to him.
He clings to those he knows
and follows strangers.
He loves the sounds
and vibrations of trains.
Unknown what his low vision
takes in, but his green eyes
draw me into mystery,
his brain a world
I can never know.

It's Not the End

My grandmother still lives in my head.
When I fell from the jungle gym,
I ran to her. "I cut my knee."
It's not the end of the world.
Over the years,
still the same answer.
"The toilet overflowed."
It's not the end of the world.
"My grandson broke his leg."
It's not the end of the world.

Today my words gush out:
"Grandma, the Pandemic is surging.
Millions of people have died.
The essential workers give more,
struggle more, die more.
The weary, the desperate stand in
food lines that stretch through
rows of shanties
or brick tenements
or fields of corn dying in its husks.
Thousands of children
sob their hunger.
The polar bears are drowning
as icebergs calve and split.
Sea waters rise through
manholes in our cities."
I am waiting for her to say it—
It's not the end of the world.

Christ in Cyberspace

What a rock show You staged!
You made the earth quake,
sent angels to tell Mary.
And where is Your son now?
Is he stranded in the Cloud,
endlessly tweeting?
Will we, Your other children,
be abandoned, spread-
eagled on atmospheric waves,
rocking toward infinity?

Free to Overlook

Gold reflects on sunset clouds,
illuminates my unruly garden,
daisies as intense as reborn sun,
evening primroses like bowls of butter,
radiant pansies, faces questioning
a softer glow, a dead sparrow,
crusted with light.
Is this light-show requiem
recompense for its rigid wings,
its silenced evening song, the loss
of its passerine passions?

Image of Your Departure

In daylight,
I crochet a shawl
that calms and holds me.
But in night's
neon-lit dreams,
you run for a train,
rush for a taxi,
race your wheelchair
after a taller,
younger woman.
You are swift
and unreachable.
I am unraveled.

Aquifer

I loved the smell of my tears
on my mother's freckled shoulder,
my dog's sleek black fur,
my father's rough sweater sleeve.

I wasted tears on broken skates,
Mrs. Miniver and *Casablanca,*
invitations that never came,
the boyfriend who didn't telephone.

Tears glued me together, washed pain
from grief, swept me back to the burden-
some business of living—my struggling
husband, a daughter who threw words, dishes.

Now my eyes are as dry as my husband's mouth.
I moisten his gums with lemon-flavored swabs
to ease him through his final hours. My well
is dry; my pump inefficient, corroded by sorrow.

Cremains

Your ashes sit on the passenger seat
as I drive west on Route Nine.
At the first traffic light, I break
the seal on the black box, remove
the plastic bag that holds them.
I read the embossed metal tag:
St. Andrew's Crematory, Number 04572.
When I stop again, I lift fine granules
that coat my hands with gray,
sniff my index finger, lick it
for the sharp clove taste of your skin,
but there is no trace of you.
I wipe my ashy hands on my skirt,
take a pinch of rosemary
from the tiny sack in my purse
that holds your wedding ring,
inhale the sharp smell of remembrance.

I will not give you to the earth
or release you to the sea.
You will stay on our bedroom dresser,
between your coin sorter and hairbrush.
Someday I will spread your ashes
on the living room floor, dance in my bare
feet, and feel you between my toes.

Touch of Love

My husband's labored breaths no longer fill the room.
In the silence I hold his hand, still warm,
familiar since our first touch, sixty years ago.

Soon the hospice nurse's bustle surrounds me.
She makes phone calls, collects medications.
I hold my husband's hand, do not move.
My daughters come with hugs and comfort.
His hand still tight in mine, I stay by his bed.

Unctuous undertakers' voices intrude,
offer condolences. When they lift
my husband, the tug
leaves me no choice. I let go.

Still, a small circle of warmth remains
in the cup of my hand.
I sit alone by his stripped bed,
staring at my palm
until the warmth
is gone.

Sometimes

Sometimes
I see the green of your eyes
between the lines of white froth
when warm waters are choppy
at St Lucia's beach.

Sometimes
I smell your tight dark curls
in the sun-touched grass
of the newly mowed meadow
where we walked on Sunday mornings.

Sometimes
I feel the elusive flutter
of your eyelashes on my cheek
and imagine I've been blessed
by the touch of a hummingbird's wing.

Never again
will my seeking toes find in the cold bedsheets
your downy calves, warm as a duckling's
new feathers. Nor will I ever hear again
the breathy sighs and murmurs of your dreams.

Word Game

If I want a night of griefless living,
I free myself from his death with words.
I start our game
in the empty silence of my mind.
I go first.
"What's the most beautiful word
in the English language?"
"Windowsill."
"No," I say, "Willow."
"Windowsill," he insists.
And I hear soft sorrowless laughter
as sleep finds me
among the repeated words:
Windowsill, Willow, Windowsill, Willow....

Morning Call

A butterfly
trembles
the door
of my dream,
swishes
the drum,
rustles
the ossicular
chain,
which thrums,
meters
the march,
Sousas me
from sleep.

Shorty's Ears

His ears, black pirate sails,
seal-slick, five inches high:
straight up now, they flopped over
till he learned to lift a leg to pee.
Inside, inky hair surrounds
three streaks of pink. I trace
one with my finger to a waxy
cave, where the mystery hides
that pivots his ears toward sound,
folds them against his head
when an eight-wheeler goes by,
opens them wide as he chases
his tennis ball with panting joy.
When I find him chewing on
my Robert Frost poems,
his ears droop in shame.
I can remember when he was a pup.*
     * *from Robert Frost, "The Span of Life"*

Snow Scene at Dawn

At dawn, my world is snow.
Silence splits, a branch

whips and snaps.

Motors grumble, plows push
piles higher than

the pompom on my hat.

Dave, my neighbor, boots to knees,

scrapes a path to the feeder, clears
feed-holes, pours in seeds for

these, the least of my creatures—

A chickadee alights on a twig;
A downy woodpecker drums

a tree trunk.

Sun brushes the maple.
Melt glistens on a bare bush,

drips.

The Rodent

When I first saw her,
she was skittering
across the hard wood floor,
a perfect match for
the snowy footprints
my daughters tracked in.
"My new pet," the youngest said.
 I grumbled, "A rodent?"

With tender claws,
the guinea pig climbed my sweater,
pressed her soft whiteness against my neck,
breathed a quiet squeak,
like a slowly opening farmhouse door.

My young daughters
shapeshifted into adolescence.
I began to notice
stealthy hints of my own aging.
I continued to grumble,
but I became the one who fed her,
cleaned her cage.

Our guinea pig did not change.
She still trundled the rounded rectangle of her body
on short dainty legs, claws lightly clicking,
shining black eyes scanning her small tranquil world.
She rattled her water bottle
when she was hungry,
and she always dropped her neat pellets
in the same corner of her cage.

I never told my family that I loved her,
let her out of the cage
when they weren't home,
fed her carrots and lettuce,
or that she found my lap while I read.

I did not tell them that sadness seeped into me
when she began to shiver and stumble.

Now I hold her in her terror,
the first time I have held death in my arms,

and I tell her I love her,
and I comfort her until she is still.

Small Outcry

The large silence of a billion snowflakes
and the small outcry of a twitting junco
are yoked to winter, hauling it toward spring.

Renegade Hand

My hand stopped listening months ago
to what I want to do.
Get out the milk is my command,
which does not matter to my hand.
It ignores the fridge and opens up
a cupboard full of fragile cups.
Sometimes it stops and hesitates,
forgets, or just procrastinates.
Do my neurons fail to communicate?
Are messages unsent or sent too late?
Perhaps my synapses are filled with sludge,
so axons and dendrites cannot budge.
What happened to the team we used to be?
My good right hand, please work with me.

Poet's Block

When the juices will not flow,
and my mind snaps shut like a frightened clam,
shall I keep on pushing a recalcitrant pen
that will not write even one iamb?

Will it take a major galactic event
with planets that twirl and realign,
so I can sit and create again
a finely metered line?

I read the greats of every ilk
to inspire metaphor or simile.
I pray to Erato, poetry muse,
who ignores my desperate plea.

Oh, please return the fertile loam
to germinate and grow a poem.

Sweet Birch

I am not as handsome
as my silvery sister
in New England.
I claimed my territory
in the dense Pennsylvania
forest by growing very tall so I could
block the sun with my wide green canopy,
and starve the ashes and the sycamores.
Now my trunk stands steady,
fastened to the forest floor
by thick twisty roots that snuffle
among rocks and chipmunk
tunnels, searching for clay hefty
enough to anchor me.

Striated plates of bark,
burnished gold, strong
as a medieval knight's armor,
guard the sapwood
that creates sweetness
within the fortress of my trunk.

But every year, prankish
spring tosses a catkin
from a wakening branch,
a yellow flower tassel
engorged with my sweet liquid,
to the softening ground.
A curious walker bites into it,
and soon *they* come with buckets.
They drill into my trunk,
insert spiles to drain my sap,
and pull off strips of bark,
leaving behind
a faint wintergreen scent.

Sometimes *they* spread
a picnic cloth in a clear spot
nearby, eat their Lebanon
bologna, their pickled eggs,
and toast with birch beer
what they have bled from me.
.

Pine

A tall pine sways against
my bedroom window.
Twig fingers tap me
from my fogged sleep.
A hat of pointed green
tilts in the autumn breeze.
Needle-fringed arms scrape
the rough red bricks
of the apartment wall.
And in the moaning wind,
I hear sighs of longing
for the mountain mother
and the fertile juices
of her loamy lap.

For the Bathroom Ant

Six legs scutter him into an alien world
of plastic and glaring light. I track him
with a hand-held spray as he tries to flee
the cascade of water, hard like a sudden storm.

The pounding stream sweeps him into the drain.
I turn off the faucet and dry my hands. An hour later
he is back on the barren expanse of vinyl floor.
Defeated, I leave, and hope he will find his way out.

He is there next morning, trying to scale the slippery
lip of the stall, but I need my morning shower.
I could kill him with my shoe, not only this small
determined life force, but thousands of his descendants.

He stops, turns his beaked face toward me. Swaying
thread-like antennae suggest he's thinking. I am mindful
that he has a brain—and a heart and a second stomach,
which carries food for the colony. I put down my shoe.

I trap him with a mouthwash cup, a skyscraper
over his triune body, carry the cup to the patio,
lean down and tip it over. He hesitates, checks
the concrete with his antennae, runs toward the grass.

The Quilter

A pattern of sturdy tissue is spread at her side
as she picks perfect squares from her memory chest.
Oiling the needle on her graying hair, she slides
it through the fragile fabric of her wedding dress.
A square from Johnny's ripped gabardines,
torn on his bike chain, is added, along with another,
cut from Jenny's prom gown of pale tangerine,
the strapless satin dress that vexed her father.
She fits a piece from a tie of her husband's family tartan
next to a square from a blue oxford shirt. A small copy
of the flag draped on Johnny's oak coffin
is stitched with the scarlet of a Flanders poppy.
Then she holds the quilt up to her face
to embroider the names time can never erase.

Restoration
> *Emptiness cannot be compressed—Kay Ryan*

No air, no wind
that whips and swirls,
nothing far; nothing near;
where a fox in
deep sleep curled,
a hawk cry told
a sparrow's fall,
deep blackness
spreads.

I sight the midline
with wet black brush,
then dip a clean
brush into white,
start two lines,
an inch apart,
angled as a path
to the vanishing point.

Burnt sienna
with yellow ochre
on my palette, I
dab at the path's
end, and two
small figures emerge
at the horizon.

Emptiness cannot be compressed.
But it can expand.

Margery Hutter Silver left her hometown in Northeast Pennsylvania for college and never returned. She and her husband settled in Boston, and she has lived in the Boston area for more than 60 years. After almost 20 years as a magazine and book editor, she studied to be a neuropsychologist and began her research on the cognitive functioning of centenarians. With Thomas T Perls, MD, she coauthored *Living to 100: Lessons in Living to Your Maximum Potential at any Age.*

In her 80s, after her retirement and her husband's death, she began to write poetry, fell in love with it, and has never stopped. Her nine decades of experience are reflected in poems about animals, nature, family, and loss, particularly the losses of old age. She experiments with different forms of poetry, such as a Villanelle or the Ghazal. "What a gift," she says, "to find a new passion for writing poetry and to have my poetry collection published at the age of ninety-two." She lives in Lasell Village in Newton, Massachusetts, near her two daughters and four grandsons.

www.ingramcontent.com/pod-product-compliance
Lightning Source LLC
Chambersburg PA
CBHW020343170426
43200CB00006B/483